Colors of CHINA

by Shannon Zemlicka
illustrations by Janice Lee Porter

Carolrhoda Books, Inc. / Minneapolis

For Papa, who made my world more colorful—S.Z.

Special thanks to Chen Chen for help with the preparation of this book.

Text copyright © 2002 by Carolrhoda Books, Inc.
Illustrations copyright © 2002 by Janice Lee Porter

This book is available in two editions:
Library binding by Carolrhoda Books, Inc., a division of Lerner Publishing Group
Soft cover by First Avenue Editions, an imprint of Lerner Publishing Group
241 First Avenue North
Minneapolis, MN 55401 U.S.A.

Website address: www.lernerbooks.com

Library of Congress Cataloging-in-Publication Data

Zemlicka, Shannon.
   Colors of China / by Shannon Zemlicka ; illustrated by Janice Lee Porter.
    p. cm. — (Colors of the world)
   Includes index.
   Summary: Explores the significance of different colors in the history, physical features, and culture of China.
   ISBN-13: 978-1-57505-478-0 (lib. bdg. : alk. paper)
   ISBN-10: 1-57505-478-7 (lib. bdg. : alk. paper)
   ISBN-13: 978-1-57505-563-3 (pbk. : alk. paper)
   ISBN-10: 1-57505-563-5 (pbk. : alk. paper)
   1. China—Juvenile literature. 2. Color—China—Juvenile literature.
[1. China. 2. Color.] I. Porter, Janice Lee, ill. II. Title. III. Series.
DS706.Z45 2002
961—dc21   99—050434

Manufactured in the United States of America
3 4 5 6 7 8 – JR – 10 09 08 07 06 05

Introduction

More than 1.2 billion people live in China, a country in eastern Asia. No other country is home to so many. Most of China's people—about nine out of ten—belong to the Han ethnic group. The rest belong to fifty-five ethnic groups scattered all over the country. China's people speak many different languages, but the country's official language is Mandarin. Its official name is the People's Republic of China.

4

Green

绿色 *Lù sè* (LOO suh)

In warm, rainy southern China, farmers tend **green** fields of rice plants. Rice needs special care to grow. Rain alone is usually not enough for the thirsty plants. They need so much water that farmers must plant rice seedlings in flooded fields called paddies. Farmers bring water to the paddies through canals and pipes. In the cooler, drier north, there is little extra water for rice. There, most farmers grow wheat.

A Chinese folk song says that rice tastes pretty good, but growing it is hard work. Can you imagine spending day after day up to your ankles in mud? Rice farmers must plant seedlings, pull weeds, keep insects away, and harvest the grain—all by hand. Machines would not do the job as well as a pair of careful hands. So the rice farmers of China work long days to feed their country.

Red

红色 *Hóng sè* (HOHNG suh)

China's flag is almost entirely **red,** the traditional color of joy and good luck. Red also stands for Communism, China's form of government. The Communist leaders try to make sure that everyone earns enough money to live. They have brought schools and electricity to places that had none. They also control where people live, what jobs they do, and who can be part of the government. They even control newspapers, radio, and television.

China has not always been a Communist country. For thousands of years, it was ruled by emperors. During this time, life was hard for many Chinese people. Some were forced to work as slaves. The emperor lost power in the early 1900s. China's government became Communist in 1949.

Many Chinese think life has gotten better under Communist rule. But others would like to choose their leaders and jobs. These people would like to earn more money than the government allows. They would also like to say and write what they think without fear of punishment.

Tan

浅褐色 *Hè sè* (HUH suh)

People travel from all over the world to see the **tan** stones of the Great Wall of China. Most of the wall was built more than five hundred years ago. A family of emperors called the Ming ruled China. The Ming were afraid of their northern enemies, the Mongols. They built many walls of stone and earth to keep the Mongols out. Over time, the walls were joined. They twisted and turned for more than four thousand miles, forming the Great Wall.

Would you like to spend your life building a wall? Thousands of Chinese did just that. They dug up the earth by hand. They baked mud bricks in hot ovens. They dragged slabs of stone for miles. But as centuries passed, the wall fell into ruins. China's leaders have begun to rebuild it as a symbol of the country's pride.

Blue

蓝色 *Lán sè* (LAN suh)

Chinese potters make **blue** and white porcelain vases, dishes, and pots. Porcelain starts as clay. It is shaped and painted, then heated in a very hot oven. How can you tell if something is made of porcelain? Strike it very gently—you'll hear a ringing sound. Chinese porcelain is made in many colors, but the beautiful patterns of blue porcelain are especially famous.

Porcelain is not only an art form. It is also one of many inventions in China's history. The Chinese were the first creators of paper, printing, gunpowder, fireworks, and even sunglasses. Many of these inventions did not reach Europe or North America until hundreds of years after their creation.

Orange

桔黄色 *Jú sè* (JOO suh)

What popular **orange** pet originally came from China? The goldfish! More than fifteen hundred years ago, Chinese fish keepers raised small, green-brown fish called carp. Carp weren't pets—they were raised for people to eat. But some were born with unusual colors. The fish keepers bred the colorful carp until silver, black, and golden orange fish were born. They were called goldfish.

Emperors and rich merchants admired the goldfish's bright colors and shiny scales. They kept them in ponds as pets. Soon many Chinese wanted pet fish. Most of them didn't have enough money or land for fancy ponds, though. In the 1200s, the Chinese began to keep goldfish indoors. Aquariums weren't made of glass in those days. Instead, goldfish lived in tanks made of clay.

13

White

白色 *Bái sè* (BYE suh)

Long winters and heavy snows make China's northern plains a hard place to live. But the Mongol people who make their homes here stay snug and warm in **white** tents called ger. Many Mongols are nomads, people who move from place to place. Mongol nomads move several times a year. They use horses to guide their herds of sheep and yaks to the grass that the animals need for food.

If you have to move a lot, it helps to have a home that can move with you. Ger are built on wooden frames. Each frame is made of several pieces, so it's easy to take apart and put together. Animal hides and felt cover the frame. A top layer of white canvas helps keep out wind and water. When it's time to move, the Mongols take apart their ger, pack them into carts, and set off across the plains with their herds.

Gold

Beautiful **gold**-colored statues fill the temples of Tibet, an area in southern China. Many of the statues show a man known as the Buddha. More than twenty-five hundred years ago, the Buddha taught that people should live peaceful, thoughtful lives. His ideas grew into a religion called Buddhism. Over many centuries, Buddhism spread throughout Asia. It became the religion of the Tibetan ethnic group and many people in other parts of China.

Tibet has not always belonged to China. Tibetans once made their own laws and lived as they wished. But in the 1950s, the Chinese army took control of Tibet. In the years that followed, the Communist government made Buddhism and all other religions against the law. People who tried to worship were punished. In the 1980s, the government began to let people practice religion again. Tibetans regained part of their old way of life. Many Tibetans hope that someday their land will again be free and at peace.

Brown

棕色 *Zōng sè* (TSOONG suh)

The **brown** waters of the Yangzi River stretch for 3,900 miles. The river starts in the western mountains of Tibet and flows to the Yellow Sea in the east. The Yangzi is the third longest river in the world. But the river is more than simply long. In the east, many fish live in the Yangzi, and the soil nearby is very good for farming. This area is called the Land of Fish and Rice.

About one-third of China's people make their homes here. Fishers catch carp, crabs, and shrimplike animals called prawns. Farmers use canals to bring water to their fields. Boats carry goods from villages to cities.

Sometimes the Land of Fish and Rice is a dangerous place. When heavy snows and rains fall, the Yangzi may rise beyond its banks. Then it may flood houses and even kill people. The Chinese have built walls of earth and stone along the river to keep the water out and their towns safe.

Black

黑色 *Hēi sè* (HAY suh)

How many **black** bicycle tires roll down the streets of Beijing every day? More than seventeen million! Most Chinese don't have enough money to buy cars. Even if they did, the streets are already jammed with taxis and buses. So most people bike, bus, or take the subway to work or school.

Beijing is a flat city, so biking isn't very hard. But if you don't want to do your own pedaling, hire a pedicab. A pedicab is a bicycle with three wheels. The driver sits up front while one or two passengers relax in the back. What if your bike or pedicab gets a flat tire? Don't worry. In Beijing, you can put air in your tires on almost every street corner. You can even have a broken bicycle fixed while you wait.

Yellow

黄色 *Huáng sè* (HWAUNG suh)

Early April is the time of the Clear Brightness Festival, a day to honor the dead. Many families bring gifts of food, flowers, and **yellow** spirit money to the graves of their ancestors, or relatives who have died. Spirit money isn't real money—it's slips of yellow paper printed with prayers. Even though the Clear Brightness Festival is a day to remember the dead, it isn't a sad day. Families sweep their ancestors' graves clean. They offer the gifts and burn the spirit money to release the prayers. Then everyone shares a picnic and flies kites.

Family life has been important in China for thousands of years. Like other parts of Chinese life, it has changed under Communist rule. Before Communism, grandparents, parents, and children often shared a single home. Modern Chinese families must fit into small apartments that the government assigns. In crowded cities, parents are allowed to have only one child. Despite these changes, the Chinese people have not forgotten their traditions. They have not forgotten to respect and honor their ancestors, the people who gave them life.

23

Index